THE FIRST EVER CHRIST...

And who to blame

Gray Jolliffe

AMBERLEY

First published 2016

Amberley Publishing
The Hill, Stroud
Gloucestershire, GL5 4EP

www.amberley-books.com

British Library Cataloguing in Publication Data.

A catalogue record for this book is available from the British Library.

ISBN 978 1 4456 6350 0 (paperback)
ISBN 978 1 4456 6351 7 (ebook)

Printed in the UK.

Of the millions of planets circling the billions of stars, in the trillions of galaxies that God had created, only the tiny planet Earth was giving him a headache.

People were ignoring the Ten Commandments. So God decided to send his only son to save them from sin.

He picked Joseph, a carpenter, and the virgin Mary to be the parents.

Soon she was pregnant, which was odd because before that a virgin couldn't be pregnant.

That December they visited the town of Bethlehem and yes, Joseph forgot to book a hotel room. So the baby arrived in a stable full of animals. But they made the best of it and soon there was quite a party, with shepherds and Wise Men and lots of singing and rejoicing.

Up till then there were no Christmas trees, no decorations, no tinsel, no houses swamped in fairy lights, no flashing Santas in sleighs, pulled by lit up reindeer.

No last minute shoppers - men in a panic and women in hysterics. Presents were unheard of, and turkeys slept the happy sleep of the unworried.

But the next day the world had changed forever.

Marketing was born.

Henceforth all mankind would receive annual gift items whether they wanted them or not.

A jolly old man called Santa Claus and his associate, a red nosed reindeer, got the Christmas gig. Which is a huge success, as you know.

And the baby Jesus?

Do you want the full story? About the details? Who said what to whom? And what whom replied? About the joy, the tears, the angst, the guilt?

Don't get your hopes up. This is only a cartoon book.

"Knock up a man's wife? What kind of angel would agree to do that?"

"Business is terrible. If I was religious I'd pray for an act of god."

"You're asking me to be a surrogate mother for no money? You're having a laugh, right?"

"It comes with the new job. Heated swimming pool. Nice, huh?"

"Of course he's gay. Do you think I'm a virgin cos I like it?"

"Not so quick, Romeo. First you have to buy me dinner."

"Beans. The secret behind reindeer flight technology."

"And you tell God you were lucky to get away with a black eye."

"It was great babe, but now I gotta fly."

"So this is where you get your red nose!"

"Actually, Mr Holier than Thou, you're just like all the others."

"Ok, pregnant is only a few lousy months, but this I have to wear all my life?"

"I can't remember the last time I heard you go Ho! Ho! Ho!"

"And here's one for the kid when it arrives – size one."

"There's just one last thing Traci. God would like you to change your name to Mary."

"Hold on Superman – you forgot one of your flip flops."

"There's something I've been meaning to share with you."

You want an iPad? Seriously? What
kind of reindeer would use an iPad?

"New gown? Different lipstick? Ok, I give up."

"I'm pregnant, you old woofter. Figure that one out."

"Tell you what Sunshine – let's have two more and miss out China."

"What do you mean I can't be? I am and you'd better get used to it."

"A pregnant virgin with a frisbee on her head. That is not normal."

"Sorry Mrs Claus, there's nobody in here fitting that description."

It's Christmas, I'm pregnant, god knows how, and now you tell me you forgot to book a room. Terrific!

"Yes sir, I can see it's a titanium credit card. But which part of 'we can only offer a cattle shed', are you failing to understand?"

"Well we'd better get this show on the road. Who's driving – you or me?"

"Christ? That's a new one – most of them put Smith."

"There's no room service, but I think there's
a mini bar under that pile of junk."

"Well don't just stand there looking at it."

"So three months ago I'm like, 'Are you sure the annexe will be finished by Christmas?' But you know builders."

Of course I still believe in God. This much chaos can't be just an accident.

"So I go out more than once a year – why the surprised look?"

"But you have to admit the conception was immaculate."

"No hurry tonight – hardly anyone's been good."

"Hurry up?? Ok, next time YOU can carry the gold."

"All this going on and you can EAT ?"

"My accountant is right. I should franchise this part of the operation."

"Jesus? Why would you want to give him a Puerto Rican name?"

"This is turning into one hell of a weird evening."

"Sorry boss, my mistake - the bicycle was for next door."

"Fat guy in a red suit, weird animal with antlers and a shiny red nose. Both looking horribly lost."

"It's our first night in the new job. Boy, what a shlep!"

"Nope - bicycles, guitars, drum kits, rowing machines but not a single full size snooker table."

"J C ? That's nice – I'm A C and he's AC/DC."

"A Capricorn yet! I too am a Capricorn. God's children, we Capricorns."

"Well I'm betting they prefer the gold to that other rubbish."

"There's a cheque for half a million in my snack box. Some poor banker must have got a cheese sandwich."

"Uh, Oh! It's at Bernie's place. Did anyone remember the Rennies?"

"WTF is THAT??"

"Yeah we found it ok. The new camels have satnav"

"Thinking about it, wouldn't it be quicker if you didn't come back up the chimney but let yourself out the front door?"

"So what were you expecting with a one star hotel?"

"And then Balthazar, in his wisdom, traded in the gold for a case of vintage claret."

"It's always tough on a kid having his birthday and Christmas all on the same day."

"Yes, I'm sure you've had no complaints,
but that's not what I meant by 'good'."

"It's supposed to be frankincense, but don't be too surprised if you find a Tonka Toy in there."

"And finally, a life subscription to his trade journal."

"It's digital you red nosed plank. You don't need to wind on."

"We have more frankincense and myrrh than we can shake a stick at. But the gold is useful."

"He's the image of his father, am I right? Look at that nose!"

"He's here to save Mankind? Well good luck, although we don't fancy his chances."

"That's right, it's my girlfriend's place. And there's no need to look at me like that."

"It's a totally new unbreakable synthetic. Go on, feel it."

"Of course it's home made. You ever tried
buying branded whisky in the bible belt?"

"Of course the real joke is he's not actually the father."

"NOW they tell us."

"Do you have any idea who that is out there? That's Mr and Mrs Christ and their baby the Saviour! And where do you put them? In the goddam stable, you Dork! I think You'd better comp us some bubbly before it gets out..."

"We must be off now. See you next Christmas maybe?"

"C'mon boss – it's gone four and we've still got Africa to do."

"Joseph, they're off at last. So I wonder if you'd get off your tush to say goodbye to these lovely gentlemen and thank them for the nice presents."

"Well that's Christmas for another year, thak heaven."

"It's the cutbacks, darling. We had to let him go."

"Not the father?" I said. "So who is – the Angel Gabriel? Oh Sure!"

"Why didn't you say you were having a Messiah?
I would have given you an upgrade."

"We'll be back around eleven, but any probs call us at Ming's Chop Suey."

"Where in God's name have you been?"

"Already he's started."

One day darling, perhaps you can work a miracle on your father.

Trade in? With 49,206,347,068,374 miles on the clock? Do me a favour.

"This is so the last Christmas I'm spending with your family."

"They even sang one called 'Camel ye Faithful'."

"So if he's just an ordinary kid what's this - a bagel?"

"And next year you take us somewhere chic, ok ? Like the Gaza Strip."

"If you'd been there, you could have had one."

"Hi guys, what's for Christmas din.....?"

"That is no carpenter. That is an intellectual!"

"It's gone out? Why - have you been a bad girl?"

"Last stop Rio. Nice planning Rudy."